Round Glasgow by Tram

Ian G. McM. Stewart

PUBLISHED BY
THE
SCOTTISH TRAMWAY MUSEUM SOCIETY

Frontispiece: The appearance of a frame from a 1902 cine film in "More Glasgow by Tram" generated such interest as to prompt illustration of another. A green car swings from Cambridge Street into Sauchiehall Street with the conductor dutifully holding the trolley rope. La Scala Picture House was yet to be built on the right.

Cover: One of Glasgow's best known landmarks is the "Hielan'man's Umbrella" in Argyle Street — a tunnel formed by the platforms of the Central Station above. It was said that highland visitors and exiles could shelter here for nothing and there has even been a song written about it. In 1956 it was a bustling place for trams too.

First published October 1979

By the same author: "Glasgow By Tram"; published 1977
"More Glasgow By Tram"; published 1978

by B. R. Chambers Ltd, Rutherglen, Glasgow, G73 1SP.
(Keighley) Limited, Chapel Lane, Keighley, West Yorkshire

INTRODUCTION

In assembling photographs for this, an unexpected third in a series of nostalgic pictures of Glasgow in the tramway period, they were "market tested" on a few friends. An architect homed in on the Charles Rennie Mackintosh buildings. A lighting engineer noticed the ornate lamp standards. Someone else spotted shoppers with paper bags in the days before carrier bags became the norm. Ladies commented on the dress hemlines. One common factor emerged; all seemed to find pleasure in these tram journeys into the secure past. Each person who browses through these pages will find what interests him.

Once more this volume has been generated from interest in its predecessors and kind readers have taken the trouble to seek out and send me their prized sepia or hand-tinted postcards and album pictures. The commercial postcard publisher of the past featured not only the obvious city centre scenes but also some of the less likely inner suburban areas. But this was before the days of urban deprivation. This was when neighbours knew each other's joys and sorrows. This was when neighbours knew each other. This was synonymous with the homely tram before Glasgow got out of "GEAR".

The late Rev. Stanley Mair of Netherlee Church once preached a sermon equating the desire for the return of old-fashioned religion with a desire for the return of the Glasgow tram. He looked straight at your author as he said this. He was later reminded that some tram enthusiasts put their cars on the same plane as religion! But this book is not only for them. It is for lovers of Glasgow, Glaswegiana and undisguised nostalgia. Enjoy these trips ROUND GLASGOW BY TRAM.

Ian G. McM. Stewart, M.C.I.B.S., M.I.Hosp.E.,
9 Blackhouse Gardens,
June 1979.   Newton Mearns, Glasgow, G77 5HS.

ACKNOWLEDGEMENTS

The author wishes to thank the following for their assistance in preparing this book: T. & R. Annan & Sons Ltd; Ian L. Cormack, M.A.; Brian T. Deans, B.A., M.Sc.; Chris K. Fletcher, R.I.B.A., A.R.I.A.S.; Hamilton Photography Ltd; Paul Hewett, F.I.E.D.; Stuart M. Little, M.C.I.T.; Brian M Longworth; Robert F. Mack; North British Traction; Brian S. Skillen, B.A.; W. A. C. Smith; Bill Tuckwell; Mrs S. Walker.

Overleaf: This is an extract from a Glasgow Corporation Transport publicity map of 1931. Comparing the fares then with those now makes a telling social comment. One thing has not changed: the leaflet stresses that services were "subject to alteration".

TRAM ROUTES

Route	Colour	Length of Route (Miles)	Time to Centre of City	Scale of Fares
(a) DALMUIR WEST AND SPRINGFIELD ROAD, (b) KNIGHTSWOOD AND AIRDRIE, via Great Western Road, Cambridge Street, St. Vincent Place and Duke Street.	Green	a 12·37 b 16·46	Dalmuir West - - 45 mins. Knightswood - - 25 mins. Airdrie - - - 60 mins. Springfield Road - 25 mins.	
(a) AIRDRIE AND PAISLEY WEST, (b) UDDINGSTON AND PAISLEY WEST, via Gallowgate, Jamaica Street and Paisley Road West.	Green	a 19·56 b 15·31	Airdrie - - - 63 mins. Uddingston - - 41 mins. Paisley West - - 41 mins.	
UDDINGSTON AND GAIRBRAID AVENUE, via Gallowgate, Glassford Street, West Nile Street, Cowcaddens and Maryhill Road.	Green	10·76	Uddingston - - 41 mins. Gairbraid Avenue - 19 mins.	
(a) CLARKSTON AND KIRKLEE, (b) LANGSIDE AND JORDANHILL, via Victoria Road, Renfield Street and Sauchiehall Street.	Yellow	a 8·68 b 6·52	Clarkston - - 30 mins. Langside - - 15 mins. Kirklee - - - 25 mins. Jordanhill - - 28 mins.	
MOSSPARK AND UNIVERSITY, via Dumbreck, Pollokshields, Renfield Street, Sauchiehall Street and Woodlands Rd.	White	6·13	Mosspark - - 24 mins. University - - 14 mins.	
(a) BURNSIDE OR (b) RUTHERGLEN AND DALMUIR WEST ; (c) AUCHENSHUGGLE AND DALMUIR WEST, via Bridgeton Cross, Argyle Street and Dumbarton Road.	Red	a 12·08 b 11·31 c 11·57	Burnside - - 26 mins. Rutherglen - - 21 mins. Auchenshuggle - 20 mins. Dalmuir West - 46 mins.	**ADULTS**
LINTHOUSE AND (a) SPRINGBURN OR (b) LAMBHILL; (c) RENFREW AND KEPPOCHHILL ROAD, via Govan Road, Paisley Road, Hope Street and Cowcaddens.	Blue	a 6·55 b 6·54 c 8·82	Linthouse - - 21 mins. Springburn - - 19 mins. Lambhill - - 18 mins. Renfrew - - 32 mins. Keppochhill Road - 16 mins.	1 Stage 2 Stages
CRAIGTON ROAD AND MILLERSTON (Change at James Street Bridge), via Govan Road, Ballater Street, Bridgeton Cross and Bellgrove Street.	Yellow	9·20	Craigton Road - 25 mins. Millerston - - 32 mins.	4 " 1 Over 4 Stages
MOUNT FLORIDA AND HILLFOOT, via Cathcart Road, Glassford Street and Maryhill Road.	Red	7·90	Mount Florida - 18 mins. Hillfoot - - 32 mins.	
SINCLAIR DRIVE AND (a) GAIRBRAID AVENUE OR (b) MARYHILL, via Victoria Road, Glassford Street and Maryhill Road.	Red	a 5·81 b 6·47	Sinclair Drive - 19 mins. Gairbraid Avenue - 19 mins. Maryhill - - 23 mins.	
RUTHERGLEN AND KIRKLEE, via Saltmarket, Hope Street, Bothwell Street and Woodlands Road.	Blue	5·74	Rutherglen - - 20 mins. Kirklee - - - 20 mins.	
RENFREW FERRY AND (a) MARYHILL OR (b) HILLFOOT, via Barrhead, Shawlands, Gorbals, St. Vincent Place and Maryhill Road.	Blue	a 19·50 b 21·34	Renfrew Ferry - 90 mins. Shawlands - - 18 mins. Maryhill - - 24 mins. Hillfoot - - 32 mins.	**JUVENILES**
MOUNT FLORIDA AND (a) PAISLEY ROAD TOLL OR (b) IBROX, via Allison Street, Nithsdale Road, Shields Road and Paisley Road West.	Yellow	a 2·56 b 3·85	Time per journey, Paisley Road Toll - 16 mins. Ibrox - - - 24 mins.	(over 5 and un 15 years of age 2 Stages 6 consecutive Stages
ROUKEN GLEN AND (a) BISHOPBRIGGS OR (b) MILLERSTON, via Shawlands Cross, Renfield Street and Parliamentary Road.	Red	a 9·50 b 10·18	Rouken Glen - 30 mins. Bishopbriggs - 25 mins. Millerston - - 28 mins.	
SPRINGBURN AND (a) MOUNT FLORIDA OR (b) NETHERLEE, via High Street and Crown Street.	White	a 4·45 b 6·30	Springburn - - 16 mins. Mount Florida - 14 mins. Netherlee - - 27 mins.	Over 6 and over 10 cons utive Stag 1¼d.
PROVANMILL AND POLMADIE, via High Street and Crown Street.	White	4·37	Provanmill - - 21 mins. Polmadie - - 10 mins.	Over 10 Stages 2
WHITEINCH AND KEPPOCHHILL ROAD, via Dumbarton Road, North Street and St. George's Road.	Green	5·26	Whiteinch - - 21 mins. Keppochhill Road - 13 mins.	
CAMBUSLANG AND ANNIESLAND, via Argyle Street, Hope Street, Bothwell Street and Crow Road.	Red	8·92	Cambuslang - - 27 mins. Anniesland - - 28 mins.	
BURNSIDE AND SPRINGBURN, via Bridgeton Cross, Bothwell Street, St. George's Road and Bilsland Drive.	White	8·80	Burnside - - 26 mins. Springburn - - 30 mins.	
RIDDRIE AND (a) SCOTSTOUN OR (b) DALMUIR WEST, via Parliamentary Road, Sauchiehall Street and Dumbarton Road.	Blue	a 7·08 b 11·05	Riddrie - - - 19 mins. Alexandra Park - 13 mins. Scotstoun - - 24 mins. Dalmuir West - 42 mins.	
CLYDEBANK AND DUNTOCHER, via Kilbowie Road.	—	2·11	Time per journey, 13 mins.	
KILBARCHAN AND RENFREW FERRY, via Johnstone, High Street, Paisley Cross and Paisley Road, Renfrew.	Green	8·74	Time to Paisley Cross. Kilbarchan - - 33 mins. Renfrew Ferry - 18 mins.	
ABBOTSINCH AND PAISLEY CROSS, via Inchinnan Road and Love Street.	—	1·47	Time per journey, 12 mins.	

By the mid 1930s the Tolbooth Steeple at Glasgow Cross had been separated from its earlier adjacent building for more than a decade. The Co-op and other premises behind the ex-Paisley tram have been razed in recent years.

Comparison of this photograph with those in the previous volumes shows that the Royal Bank building at the corner of Candleriggs and Trongate has been reduced in height by two storeys. The cupboard recesses high up on the gable wall of the adjacent building are still evident.

Finnieston Cross in the 1880s. While the shops have become more cosmopolitan since this picture was taken, the odd indentation of the tenements remains today where Kent Road on the left enters Argyle Street.

St Vincent Place tramway station and siding is shown in 1895 with the fine banking hall of the Clydesdale Bank on the right. Fortunately the site survived plans for a high rise development and the building has been refurbished and stone-cleaned.

When Jamaica Bridge was rebuilt and widened during the mid-late 1890s, a temporary "accommodation" bridge was constructed alongside. The horse trams were diverted on to it as well as all the other traffic, as can be seen from this archive photograph.

The Union Street–Argyle Street crossing was pounded by trams for twenty hours of every day of every year. The track latterly installed there has been laid to rest at the Wakebridge terminus of the Crich Tramway Museum.

This view of Stockwell Street at Argyle Street corner was one of a portfolio taken to justify the need for what later emerged as George V Bridge. This is 17th April 1914 at 4.50 pm but nothing seems to hurry the horse and cart making economic use of the tram lines, saving time, energy, bumps and noise.

A busy Argyle Street scene photographed in 1928 when public transport took trade right to the shop doors like those of the barber's on the extreme left. But where have the people gone? Cumbernauld, East Kilbride, Castlemilk . . .

This part of Sauchiehall Street is now traffic free and has seen much new building construction. Reid and Todds is still there but Muirheads has gone to be replaced by a modern Boots store — their third premises in the street within the last twenty years! The photo dates from 1939.

The trams generated their own industry and a special breed of men fabricated and installed the rails and pointwork. Here is the Barrland Street Permanent Way yard around 1913.

Trams on service 30 ran virtually through the middle of a steelworks in Glasgow's east end. This is Beardmore's Parkhead Forge. A small boy is taking the baby out for a cough in the pram.

John Brown's Shipyard at Clydebank was the birthplace of the Cunard "Queens" and many other famous ocean liners. This is the yard gate around 1910 with a "red" tram awaiting lunchtime passengers.

While Springburn was the premier district for the railway industry there was also the Dubs Works in Polmadie, inevitably provided with an adjacent tram terminus. This is a commercial postcard view which well illustrates the size of the locomotive works.

TRAMS AND CHURCHES

Dumbarton Road at Partick is still quite recognisable despite the seventy years which have elapsed since this view was recorded by Annan's camera. The left-hand pavements have narrowed, those on the right are wider and Newton Place Church now has a clock without hands.

Great Western Road at the St George's Cross end illustrates the spire of St Mary's Cathedral near the camera and further distant the very slender spire of Lansdowne Church at Kelvinbridge. This latter was once one of Britain's tallest. "Better steeples than multi-storey flats . . ."

Maitland Street provided a terminal spur for trams from the north of the city, also housing trolleybuses. Notice the "Jenny a'things" store and Cowcaddens Free Church, the building of which is now associated with the Theatre Royal at the top of Hope Street.

The tram is crossing from Bothwell Street into Elmbank Street at their junction with St Vincent Street. This area has been greatly transformed by the M8 motorway and its deceleration lanes but the Alexander "Greek" Thomson Church still dominates the scene.

13

Sauchiehall Street theatreland in 1915. The tram heading north plastered with Army recruiting posters is about to pass the Pavilion Theatre while the other waits between the Empire and the Lyric.

The same junction during a murky day in December 1944 shows a serviceman taking his chance to cross between the trams with their white fenders, headlamp masks and darkened interiors.

14

Driver Alexander Grant served the Tramways Department for 33 years from 1905 based at Maryhill Depot. He is shown with his tram in Clincart Road, Mount Florida, accompanied by a tartan-skirted conductress keeping war services running in 1917.

This comes from an early lantern slide of Keppochhill Road with the original Springburn Depot. Sighthill Cemetery is behind the "Room and Kitchen" tram. The first power station was adjacent to the depot and the plant was sold to the Rothesay Tramways when Pinkston was commissioned.

High Street in 1899 with Glasgow Cathedral shrouded in fog. Notice the appalling road surface and the mud-spattered dash on the tram — a testimony to an early decision to paint these panels dark brown. The brae here ruled out horse traction and tramway service opened with these electric cars.

This is the former Hutcheson's Grammar School in Gorbals. This school — affectionately known as "Hutchie" — now maintains a fine reputation for academic achievement in new premises near Crossmyloof Ice Rink.

The High School of Glasgow has been reopened at Old Anniesland as a private venture by its former pupils following the Corporation's closure of the Elmbank Street buildings on the right. These were where the author "educated" his teachers on trams like 488 now preserved in Paris.

Gorbals Cross in 1917 shows tenement buildings with more of Alexander Thomson's Grecian detailing. They have been demolished along with property on the other three sides of the Cross and the new Gorbals therefore has no heart like the old.

Finnieston Cross in 1956 should be compared with the view of the same location on page 6. The 16 tram is on the unusual turning loop commencing its return journey to Possilpark Depot.

St George's Cross at the junction of Great Western Road and Maryhill Road in the 1930s before this intersection was downgraded in importance with the construction of the bypassing M8 motorway. Whatever happened to Ross's Dairies?

Anniesland Cross around 1936. There was still much housing to be built in Temple and traffic was sparse. The Crow Road tram terminus is at the foot of the picture with the Old Anniesland Playing Fields on the left. A mission tent can be seen on its regular corner site.

If London has water buses, Glasgow had the "Cluthas" and this one is about to pass beneath the original Caledonian Railway Bridge into Central Station with Jamaica Bridge beyond complete with open top tramcar. Tramway competition ended the river service in 1903.

Partick Bridge over the Kelvin, embellished with the former Burgh's coat-of-arms which is not generally noticed by the passing public. Behind the tram in this 1961 view is the Partick Sewage Pumping Station.

Judging by the crowds leaning over the ballustrade at George V Bridge one of the L.M.S. Pleasure Steamers is about to leave Bridge Wharf on a trip "Doon the water". This is 1938, year of the Empire Exhibition at Bellahouston Park.

Crow Road has become the main northern approach to the Clyde Tunnel and now has to deal with considerably more traffic than a 17 tram placidly heading south for Broomhill Cross and Partick in 1955. Scotland's "other national drink" is still with us, even if advertising styles have changed.

A depot-bound tram passes Maryhill Central station on the left and the oft-remembered Maryhill Barracks of the Highland Light Infantry. Nowadays only the wall remains, enclosing the Wyndford housing scheme.

Grosvenor Terrace at Botanic Gardens had one of the most splendid facades in Glasgow but a major fire destroyed the Hotel portion nearest Byres Road. Fortunately the Grosvenor did not suffer the fate of fire-razed Botanic Gardens Station buildings and modern materials enable reproduction of the original to overlook the empty site opposite.

Glasgow Cross and Tron Steeple

The Caledonian Railway's Glasgow Cross Station was a mixture of Roman and Baronial architecture with lots of cast iron. The opulence of the structure was in stark contrast with the smoke-filled hell-hole below.

Overleaf: Cheap fares encouraged patronage. This dictated improved services which dictated more patronage which dictated further improved services which dictated cheaper fares. Look at Trongate, full of busy trams. This is not even the rush-hour!

The stations of the original Glasgow Underground were diminutive and difficult to find but had a character all their own. The modernised stations could only be an improvement even if they are not the same! Notice the "Subway" Bar, perpetuating the unofficial name of Glasgow's "toy railway" at Cowcaddens.

Bridge Street Subway Station offered a larger frontage to its potential travelling public before its demolition anticipated modernisation. Again, there is an adjacent bar, paired like Castor and Pollux (or Woolworths and Marks & Spencers!).

Howard and Wyndham's King's Theatre with a tram going to "Barracks Gate". Jack House recalls that the Glasgow comedian Tommy Morgan once claimed that he could do 19 weeks in a different theatre every week, all reached by Glasgow tramcar.

A famous Glasgow nightspot of "Come Dancing" fame was the Locarno. It also used to run lunchtime dancing sessions to gramophone records in the fifties — an early version of the disco?

This is Eglinton Toll many years before the traffic barrier was installed. A dentist still occupies the first floor premises in the building on the left (not the same gentleman . . . !).

If you were to ask a Glaswegian "Does this tram go to the Plaza?" the inevitable raucous retort would be "Naw, it disnae dance". This is dancing tramcar No. 481 outside the Plaza at Eglinton Toll in September 1955 — even today a Mecca (sorry!) for ballroom dancers.

No sooner was the statement made in "More Glasgow by Tram" that few photographs seemed to exist of Crown Street than T. & R. Annan turned up this one. It is gratefully published showing an 1899 Sunday scene. Govan Street crosses in front of the camera and the Justiciary Buildings are in the distance, left, across Albert Bridge.

Nelson Street, Tradeston, under the Central Station approach railway bridge. The tram beyond is emerging from Commerce Street — often announced by conductresses as "C'merce Street".

West End shopping in Byres Road was a quiet affair in Edwardian times before the expansion of the Glasgow University campus and the coming of the B.B.C., just up the road at Queen Margaret Drive.

Two young Sunday cyclists watch a Coronation tram passing them at the Hyndland Road shops near Clarence Drive in April 1957. There is something timeless about Hyndland and it still looks substantially the same now.

The mounting of the 1959 Scottish Industries Exhibition was the last occasion when the Transport Department provided an illuminated tram to tour the night time streets. This had been a long-standing tradition in Glasgow. This car was one of the Works fleet suitably disguised.

A lively scene outside the Kelvin Hall recalls the Exhibition itself. The buildings of the Western Infirmary and the closely linked Glasgow University are in the background segregated from Kelvingrove Park by the River Kelvin.

The Half-Way House, Glasgow and Paisley

The Halfway House (between Glasgow and Paisley) in 1906. Only the building to the immediate right still stands while the Halfway House Bar has been superseded by a supermarket and shopping development built around the inevitable high flats.

The same spot in 1955 looking towards town with Bellahouston Park in the distance. Mosspark Boulevard leads off to the right of the tram.

Paisley Road, Ibrox.

The sweeping arc of Alexander Thomson's Walmer Crescent, Cessnock, could be favourably compared with the architecture of Bath or Cheltenham but the view from Paisley Road West was soon ruined by the construction of single-storey shops along their frontage.

Time to catch up with the day's events as three city-bound trams approach Paisley Road Toll along Paisley Road West at Plantation. Most of the streets to the left and right have been closed off in this redeveloping district.

A view of London Road just before it enters the former Burgh of Calton east of Glasgow Cross. In 1915 it was still named London Street. The tram is passing Moir Street on the right where a run-round loop was later installed to alleviate traffic disruption in the City Centre.

Old Pollokshaws at Greenview Street in 1954 illustrates buildings since demolished although part of the Town's House survives. This single track was used only for depot workings. The two little girls are obviously out in their "Sunday Best".

Here is an 1888 view of Govan Road from a tenement in Carmichael Street looking on to the site later occupied by the dry dock. In the distance, right, is "The Gloaming" — later Princes Dock. The road now has to take an avoiding right turn just at the spot where the steam tram can be seen.

Golspie (formerly White) Street, Govan, where the approaching No. 7 tram is about to negotiate a seemingly never-ending succession of right-angled bends at ever-increasing speeds before it reaches its Jura Street terminus.

This is the Newlands end of Kilmarnock Road, Shawlands, which in pre-World War I days had its own cluster of shops quite remote from those at Shawlands Cross. Now they are combined in an extensive and comprehensive shopping area.

The Wolseley saloon seems set to knock down two unsuspecting ladies. Not really, as this was a safety-first propaganda effort. Out of the picture on the right, an inspector is keeping oncoming traffic at bay from this Kilmarnock Road "film set".

One of the Corporation's traditional practices was to erect two handsome lamp posts outside the homes of their Lord Provosts. These belonged to Sir Myer Galpern and were in Nithsdale Road, Pollokshields.

No energy problems at Mount Florida terminus in 1956 as a lonely tram is about to be overtaken by an advancing army of trolleybuses on Cathcart Road. Despite their introduction as recently as 1949, trolleybuses outlived the trams by only five years.

RENFREW TO MILNGAVIE

This is the War Memorial at Renfrew near the terminus of the Renfrew Ferry to Milngavie service — once the longest in Britain at nearly twenty-three miles. Two return trips filled up a complete shift for platform staff!

The tram terminus at Milngavie was just short of the town being just beyond the Bearsden boundary. This 1954 view was taken at Park Road near the terminus to which the number 29 tram has journeyed all the way from Glasgow's East End.

Building construction and maturing trees now prevent this aspect of Paisley's George A. Clark Town Hall being caught by the camera. This is 1935 with a Young's bus and Corporation tram competing for customers.

This was taken from a tram heading down Graham Street for Airdrie Cross and shows an impatient S.M.T. bus. The small-town character of Airdrie has not entirely disappeared since 1953, despite rebuilding on the left which has included removal of the former Caledonian Railway East Station.

Track repairs in the post-war years were still carried out in much the same way as in early days. Technology had not advanced much and the familiar tar boiler was part of the city scene. Anniesland Cross is in the distance behind the waiting tram.

A suburban scene at Knightswood Cross. The central reservation for trams survives, infilled, crying out for their return.

The service from Duntocher to Clydebank ran up and down Kilbowie Road. The termini were in contrast to each other; industrial Clydebank above and rustic Duntocher below. Such was the descent into Clydebank that these trams exhausted all the air from their cylinders in brake applications until larger reservoirs were installed shortly after the route was opened in 1924.

Main Street, Cambuslang

Cambuslang was once known as the largest village in Scotland. Here is its Main Street in Edwardian days with a "red" tram bound for Stobcross Ferry.

Kilbarchan was undoubtedly the furthest west you could reach by Glasgow tramcar. Once part of the Paisley system, the route was restricted to these anachronistic open-toppers by a low bridge at Elderslie. This rare photo was taken on the last day of trams in May 1932 before conversion to Corporation buses.

Large private housing estates have been constructed around Bishopbriggs and nearby Lenzie such that the Kirkintilloch Road now carries greatly-inflated traffic flows. Here is the Kenmure Avenue tram terminus. The town centre shops now extend to both sides of this junction.

Tramcar 1000 at Clarkston Toll in 1952 is seen before the construction of the roundabout and the brief reign of the replacement trolleybuses. The serenity of the scene is in stark contrast with the private motor traffic of today.

RURAL TRAMS

Garrowhill in the 1950s retained an almost rural atmosphere, emphasised by the rustic farm cart hugging the hedgerows on the left.

The tram on the country single-track section has just come past the foot of Gleniffer Braes as it travelled between Glenfield and Cross Stobs. Movement of trams on this one-mile portion was controlled by signals and one can be seen mounted on the pole on the right.

A foretaste of the current enthusiasm for nostalgia was evident in the 250,000 turn-out for the closing procession of Glasgow's trams seen here passing Lewis's on 4th September 1962. These trams survive today but, let it be whispered, the horses had to be brought from Edinburgh!

Now in the Glasgow Museum of Transport Collection, tram 1088 is seen here newly outshopped heading down Cumbernauld Road near Warriston Street. Contrary to the traffic sign, city-bound trams followed their own lane discipline.

Bridgeton Cross is the setting for another survivor. 585 is now displayed in London's South Kensington Science Museum. The bowed and bent bodywork was suitably straightened before it left Glasgow on its longest-ever trip. Behind the tram is the former North British Bridgeton Central Station.

Notice the detail on the bow-windowed tenements in Kenmure Street, Pollokshields. Buildings such as these were not "flung up" in times past. Neither was the tram: this 1900 veteran survives and runs at the Crich Tramway Museum.

Bothwell Street was the home of the prestige car showrooms. This photograph was taken in 1959 some years before George and Jobling found their habitat in Possilpark. St Vincent Street Church is high up on the right and survives still, like this particular tramcar.

This part of Argyle Street is now traffic-free with a modern imitation of cobbled setts. The Argyle Picture House was offering continuous performances from 11.00 am. Tram 1297 now offers continuous performances at the Crich Tramway Museum.

For many, the Glasgow tramcar will recall joyful times and a view of a handicapped children's outing to Rouken Glen in 1936 makes a happy ending to this book.

PHOTOGRAPHIC CREDITS

Photographs used in this book have come from the following sources and are gratefully acknowledged. The term "collection" has been used where there was no identification to enable full credit to be given.

T. & R. Annan & Sons Ltd: 12a, b, 29a.

P. F. Bloxam Collection: 9b, 23b.   W. A. Camwell: 41b.

Ian M. Coonie: 46b.   R. R. Clark: 34b, 38b.

G.C.T. Collection: 10a, 16a, 40a, 48.   The "Glasgow Herald": 45a.

Wm Grant: 15.   R. L. Grieves Collection: 11b, 23a.

R. Hogg Collection: 36a.   Lens of Sutton Collection: 28a, 37b.

Neil M. Lawrence: 20b.   Brian M. Longworth Collection: 38a, 41a.

R. F. Mack: 29b, 33b, 35b, 40b, 44a, 47a, b, back cover.

W. D. McMillan: 17b, 22a, 28b.   W. F. McWhirter Collection: 8a.

N.B. Traction: 5, 9a, 11a, 14a, b, 17a, 19a, 21, 27a, 30a, 33a, 42a.

Dr Hugh Nicol: 44b.   A. D. Packer: 46a.   People's Palace Collection: 7b.

S.T.M.S. Collection: cover, 3, 13b, 18b, 24/25, 30b, 32b, 36b, 39a, b, 42b, 43b.

David E. Sinclair: 31a.   Brian S. Skillen Collection: 32a.

W. A. C. Smith: 13a, 22b, 26a, b, 31b, 37a.   W. A. C. Smith Collection: 6a, b.

Strathclyde Regional Archives: 7a, 8b, 16b, 18a, 20a, 34a, 35a.

Alastair Stirling: 10b.   T.M.S. Archives: frontispiece.

Valentine, Dundee: 19b, 27b, 43a.   R. J. S. Wiseman: 45b.

BLOCKS. Generous contributions towards the cost of blockmaking have been made by the following S.T.M.S. members:

David S. Brown 12b, 28b, 40a, 42b; Ian L. Cormack 42a; Brian T. Deans 30b; John G. Fender 40b; Robert L. Grieves 38a; David Henderson 19a; Colin B. Lees 41b; Stuart M. Little 38b; Brian M. Longworth 17a; Tom Quinn 41a; Alan Ramsay 22a; David E. Sinclair 6b, 43a; Ian Stewart 17b, 33a; Iain M. Terrace 11a.